DARK WOODS

DARK WOODS

RICHARD SANGER

BIBLIOASIS
WINDSOR, ON

Library and Archives Canada Cataloguing in Publication

Sanger, Richard, 1960-, author
    Dark woods / Richard Sanger.

Poems.
Issued in print and electronic formats.
ISBN 978-1-77196-232-2 (softcover).--ISBN 978-1-77196-233-9 (ebook)
    I. Title.

PS8587.A3723D37 2018   C811'.54   C2017-907002-9
                                                 C2017-907003-7

Edited by Zachariah Wells
Copy-edited by Emily Donaldson
Typeset by Ellie Hastings
Cover designed by Chris Andrechek

Canada Council for the Arts / Conseil des Arts du Canada — Canada — Ontario (Ontario Media Development Corporation) — ONTARIO ARTS COUNCIL / CONSEIL DES ARTS DE L'ONTARIO (an Ontario government agency / un organisme du gouvernement de l'Ontario) — FSC — MIX Paper from responsible sources — www.fsc.org — FSC® C004071

Published with the generous assistance of the Canada Council for the Arts, which last year invested $153 million to bring the arts to Canadians throughout the country, and the financial support of the Government of Canada. Biblioasis also acknowledges the support of the Ontario Arts Council (OAC), an agency of the Government of Ontario, which last year funded 1,709 individual artists and 1,078 organizations in 204 communities across Ontario, for a total of $52.1 million, and the contribution of the Government of Ontario through the Ontario Book Publishing Tax Credit and the Ontario Media Development Corporation.

PRINTED AND BOUND IN CANADA

in memory of
Penny (Ketchum) Sanger
18 March 1931–13 July 2017

Table of Contents

DARK WOODS

Outside In

Inside, air, breath, song, the very element
you move in and hold on to, still: vain aspiration.

Outside, jackhammers, diesel fumes assail the senses,
newsprint and grime age and adhere to you,
your wrinkles, yes, and crevices—
all that, and time, your time here, which presses,
drives you north, fleeing smog, brown-outs,
new games and gizmos, parties and prizes,
coffee lids cartwheeling in the ditch,
the whole noisy world that charges on regardless,

till here you are, on the shore of a lake
with nothing to go on but the bone-chilling water
that dares you and this heaving in your breast:
heart, soul, what have you…   You take a breath,
take this sample of your time, random particles
of this and that, noble gases, exhaust,
you grab like a thief grabs a handbag,
like the lungful your life depends on, and plunge.

Artichoke

Handsome knob, armadillo, hand-grenade
of army green, armour-plated petals,
man enough to top a column
or stop a banister dead in its tracks,
you were never meant to open up and flower,
let alone explode and rejoice,
never scatter, amidst hosannas, your seed—
no, not in this barren world at least.
Here your lot is to keep it in,
to remain tight-lipped and celibate,
nodding your bald pate wisely at the rumour
of pleasures you shall never taste—

the pleasures we have to drag out of you,
by teaching you to be tender, to share
with us your innermost feelings.
First, we apply boiling water,
then the full treatment:
one by one, I rip each petal
from your heart like a confession
I'll savour and discard, like a tongue
whose root I've torn and streaked,
as I tug and drag it out over my teeth.

Babble

Born but never gone back to that cottage
your parents, clueless, rented in the mining village
where running water meant a stream and buckets;
the cottage your father would have to leave,
to go, quickly abroad, as men did in those days,
and your mother—young, untested, Canadian—
tried to cope: two boys to nurse, coal fire to tend,
laundry to do, to dry, the useless little jars,
the sour chemist who mocked her accent,
and all the things a mother had to do;
never back to the garden she left untended that spring,
the hedges unkempt, moss and vines gone wild,
creeping over the cobbles, up the brick, tut-tut,
where once after lunch she would set you and your twin
in the sun, imagine that, the sun, to nap
beneath the nappies on the line, and as you slept,
you heard, didn't you, somewhere off
beyond the end of the garden, the babble of a stream
swollen with April showers, that came from way back
in the hills and was old as them, this stream
that laughed and gurgled and ran through the country,
collecting everything it heard, swear words, slang,
sweet nothings, flowing downriver and out
into the ocean, and the mouths of the world,
to pray and curse and sing and barter on the tongues
of pilgrims, sailors, swordsmen, and slave traders,
dock-workers, journalists, left-at-home mothers,
and one day to babble on your untutored tongue too.

Dark Woods

Bedtime, lights out and book dispatched
to the landslide on the floor, along with toy cars
and hockey cards, I lie beside my son in the dark,
the two of us looking up, heads on one pillow,
reviewing the places we've been, or want to go,
—Oxtongue Lake, the Rockies, Timbuktu—
the best times of year to be there (the fall, the monsoons).
We sip each place-name and sigh in agreement,
our little talk fading to reverie,
to silence as, half a block away,
the Dundas streetcar clatters to a stop,
disgorging its cargo of partygoers,
and slowly, slowly he begins our night-time ritual
intoning the words of an old poem
about the woods and snow. It's November
in a little bedroom in downtown Toronto,
and next door, I know, in the rooming house,
the men are getting ready to go out
to their dishwashing jobs on Spadina Avenue.
We lock our bicycles to the same poles
and at night sleep within feet of each other
separated only by the plaster
and timbers of these hundred-year-old rowhouses—
our dreams swelling in separate compartments
and never meeting. Everything I think I know
about them could be wrong. It's November
and on this side of the wall, we look forward
to the snow, listening to the words
of an old poem that, for all I know,
embodies everything our neighbours wished to flee,
that quaint image of the puzzled horse

stopping by those snowy woods (which someone owns)
recalling nothing so much as the pictures
on the maple syrup tins we buy.
Or would they recognize those woods as the same
that the poet Han Shan took refuge in
on Cold Mountain? And the little horse
the pale descendant of a Mongol stallion?

Whoever owned those woods will have sold them,
and they've probably built a subdivision there,
or retirement community, with two-car garages,
hedges and scrawny transplanted trees,
and in the woods that are left, it's not horses
or harness bells but skidoos and their roar
that will disrupt the evening, and the sleep
of all the little creatures tucking in,
the acrid smell of those engines lingering
to remind us just how much the poem leaves out.
And yet the words follow one another
as sure as footsteps, and he recites them
with such tenderness, such trust,
the simple incantation draws me in
and I know, for the seventh time in his short life,
he's imagining the snow arriving,
spinning in the air outside his window,
falling on the ledge, and on the boughs
of the pines and cedars in those dark woods
the poem can't stop telling us about.

Halfway through my life, I find myself
in the dark with this little boy
beside me. There are so many things
I don't know as I attempt to guide him
through the world, I might as well be lost

in some dark forest, clad in mammoth furs
like a primeval hunter-gatherer
who clutches an infant to his breast
for warmth, murmuring this tribal spell
to allay and contain the shadows growing
amongst evergreens. Who sleeps next door?
What weather will the sky tomorrow bring?
Why does that man have pale blotches on his face?
What will we eat? I don't know, I can't know,
all I can do, the sum of my knowledge,
is whisper the next word if he falters.
Next door, there's a wheeze and a cough,
the floorboards creak, the streetcar starts up
and through the snow we're looking forward to,
we march on, one simple word at a time,
a smile on his face at the thought of it,
his little hand letting go of mine,
miles to go, miles to go... And he's asleep.

The Family Racket

1: Reading

He's just started to read, so I give him the sports
from the thin, thin *Globe* we get each morning
and, as I wrestle with breakfast and coffee,
he spreads out his paper on the living-room carpet
and, slowly sounding out the name of each city,
tells me who won: Chicago, Ottawa,
Toronto… Then one evening I bring home the *Star*
and, as I unpack groceries and open wine,
he flips its pages and groans: Dada, what cheaters!
It's a new paper but they've copied the same scores.

2: Writing

I write, and now, at the kitchen table, my son,
age six, announces he will too, calling
like some blonde princeling for a pen and paper.
To him, it's something I, and, by extension,
all grown-ups do, something he figures
he's old enough to start. And it's shaping the letters,
making circles, attaching trunks or tails, crosses, dots,
that absorbs him, thumb pressed hard, tongue stuck out.
The words themselves don't seem to matter much,
there are so many out there, floating around,
he's happy just to pull one out of the air,
get it down on paper, and show it to me:
one word, one reader, just enough to set
the whole damn racket going once again.

The Way It Worked

One crossed glance, her wet eyelashes dip and up
she gets, hips negotiating an exit
through chairs and tables till, outside the bar, party, café,
this tomboy who's caught your eye, lithe and insouciant,
and whom—after the properly stipulated delay—
you follow out, looks away
from her circle, and smiles back shyly,
smiles again and now with raw, inquisitive eyes
meets your gaze and holds it... And you look back,
and you look, like a diver afraid to plunge
into those dark pools, afraid to drown,
then, as if it had never been done before,
you pull out a smoke and saunter up to ask
—*¿Tienes fuego? As-tu du feu? Hast du Feuer?*—

*

A sardonic twist to her grin, her hand
wriggling into her jeans to dig out a Bic
and flick... Behold the old ritual:
Watch the tip catch and glow, the smoke rise
and disperse among the stars above.
What will you find to keep the spark alight?
What music, home towns? What zodiac signs?

Blind Tom

"At one lecture, in Edinburgh again, a former colleague, Tom Creighton, rose to his feet to protest after a peculiarly challenging exposition of new Continental thinking: 'It's all higher froggy nonsense, isn't it Frank?'... Who knows, had he his century he might have come to love Thomas Hardy."

—John Sutherland on Frank Kermode,
The Guardian, 21 August 2010.

Those great eyebrows swooping like birds of prey
round your cramped digs in Buccleuch Place,
the wild gorse-bush of hair, the fogged-up lenses
that slid down that craggy, dripping face
as you tried to fix your dull gaze on a voice
and see the point of the duller things we said:
vague, nebulous clay you had to tutor
on Milton and Donne and work into shape
such as you might one day have full sight of
in heaven, or Wessex, or wherever...
"The English have no passion," I opined,
callow, ignorant, unread. A cheap shot,
and easy enough to fire off in Scotland.
You rose in a moth-eaten cardigan,
I kid you not, to whack clean your pipe
on the coal-fire grate, and tried to be polite.
"Quite" or "rather good" was how you praised.
I wanted unqualified certainties,
the truth in black and white. You read our essays
in the bath, apologized for splotches,
and had to defend Hardy to the toff
who claimed "The Darkling Thrush" was wet.
When I championed Othello (plus Hamlet)

against Eliot's "emotion in excess"
—standard first-year essay fare—you digressed,
recalling how, in Uganda, you'd played the part,
a white soldier-prof surrounded by black:
"It is the cause, it is the cause... chaste stars!"
your voice rumbled, wracked with all the feeling
you could wring from English, the smart of battles
I never knew you'd fought. I had no idea.

Some Blessed Hope
(for Bruce Taylor)

To tell the truth, to pull
the bowstring taut and feel
that catgut, those sinews
shed all flesh, all fat,
to disdain, nay, eschew,
yes, *eschew* all ornament,
extraneous arabesque,
to wait patiently until
you hit upon the word
you need, like a weapon,
and match it to your task,
draw the string slowly back
amid the mindless chatter,
pause an endless second,
then dispatch that arrow
in one immaculate arc,
perfectly calibrated,
and impale, *oh mot juste*,
there, on the trembling branch,
the songbird's warbling heart.

Rain

Rain, a drop, on the open page, now two,
    of the book you read this afternoon by a northern lake,
    now a splatter, wetting the rough old paper
    and this smooth young hero who dons his cape, and steps out into—
Rain in the distant Isles,
    on the country houses, the housing estates,
    the cottages, on rose gardens and hedgerows
    of boxwood and yew releasing their scent,
    on the woolen uniforms of little boys
    who, through rising damp and mouldy leather satchels,
    grew up to settle down on tropical plantations,
    rubber-tapping capitalists who would invent
    the Wellingtons and Mackintoshes to defeat, they thought—
Rain in the orchards of Montauban, Niagara and the Okanagan
    you disappeared into for the summer
    to make your fortune, on the leaves of peach trees
    whose boughs sunk under the weight
    of the fruit and the wet, and on the mud beneath
    you had to walk through, as best you could, to the truck,
    lugging the over-full trays of fruit you picked,
    your boots sinking, squelching, then stuck,
    your sock foot escaping, you hopping, cursing—
Rain going pitter-pat on the lead-mullioned windows
    a young man sits at and now looks through to see
    a robin picking its way across the green quad,
    examining like print the blades of grass
    as the man's fingers on the typewriter keys
    pause and then go pitter-pat—
Rain on the doormats of West Berlin
    stomped, shaken off, seeping into the sisal
    on which, *aus aktuellen Anlassen,*

—because of present conditions—
they asked you to leave your boots, your shoes,
and you went inside, sock-footed,
to try out the new words on your tongue
half-lives and becquerels and a place called Chernobyl
then felt them seep into your talk,
as everyone waited for the sun that would disperse—
Rain on the surface of the lake
at the end of summer, prickling like a rash,
as a late band of mosquitos congregates
in the cedars plotting their next offensive
and the children gather indoors
round a board to plot theirs,
oblivious to how plans, conditions change,
things can happen, for example—
Rain interrupt your life at moments,
making the asphalt surface, say, slick and oily
the car then swerve, lives change course like that,
no pattern but this random collision
of low pressure and cold fronts now splattering the page
of the book you happen to be reading
whose hero, having met his first reverse,
now pauses to read, say, some lines
and perhaps deviate from the path
he will no doubt resume, a path that's straight
and true, so unlike—
Rain falling slant, haphazard,
in blotches on the old paper
and then in a rush on the page
you have open (page 62)
a moment you might surmise when clouds gathered, or sorrows,
and drops fell, the way they do,
Rain or tears, welling up this afternoon
with little warning but that smell that comes before,

tarmac or pine resin, the earth opening its pores,
    the hero pausing, you reading, and suddenly—
Rain pouring down in torrents, in big fat drops,
    everything you have lost or forgot,
Rain falling slant through your life, falling true,
Rain passing,
Rain past,
Rain you remember does not remember you.

Europe by the Back Door
(for Christopher Clark)

Disembarking before dawn at Heathrow
or the Gare du Nord, marching backpacks crammed
with sacred texts up the great boulevards
to breakfast like Beckett's tramps on stale croissants,
we attacked the old continent head-on:
Eurail Pass—check. Swiss Army Knife—check.
Camus, Joyce, Kafka—check, check, check. Barthes—check.
Vergangenheitsbewältigung…? Not yet.
Thirty years later, rushing through the dark
of Istanbul to catch the last ferry west
to Kabatas, to Kadakoy, to Europe—damn it!—
we were slipping in, as real refugees do,
through the back door: Would the old lady not
sigh a little and adjust her rear for us
as the frisson passed? We charged aboard,
and snagged the choicest seats—outside, lower deck—
just as we'd once met and quickly collapsed
beside each other on the Berlin U-Bahn.
You quoted Larkin then. Now we were dads,
Lebenskunstler who'd really fucked it up,
looking out across the dark Bosphorus
at bright Europe as the seagulls cawed
and a ferry-horn sounded. Faint makeshift lights
strung from invisible boats criss-crossed our bow
and ahead all of Sultanahmet glowed:
Topkapı Palace, Aya Sofia, the Blue Mosque,
Oh holy city of Byzantium!
Hookahs and harems of Constantinople!
This was the continent we'd dreamt of
lifting her skirts for us, and her mysteries,

as midnight grew near. This is life, I thought,
the bracing sea-breeze, the muezzins' distant blare,
the million things we talked and laughed about,
all of Tarlabaşi ahead of us...
Then the sky went dark. Like that.
Was this history, all the lamps going out,
Europe and our hopes for her extinguished
in a flash? Would we founder here and drown
like so many? The dark moved. We looked up.
The penny dropped. We were ships in the night:
ours, a two-decker passenger ferry,
and this, a huge Russian container ship
gliding out of the Black Sea, seven storeys high,
silent, taking something somewhere
but not inclined to tell us what, or why.

Thrown

Thrown for a moment, that's all,
the same slight wooziness you feel
when the floor your foot expected falls
suddenly away, and your knee buckles—
or picking up the drink you've nursed for hours,
you realize, since it, too, has sunk
to a new level, either someone's drunk
from your glass—or you're walking off with theirs.

Merrily Down the Stream

Like the rivers we canoe, the Rideau, the Jock,
the Ottawa, our lives, calm and composed
in their stately progress through the landscape,
spreading out to collect the tributes due
and grow, acquiring girth, momentum, gravitas,
just the occasional wobble, nothing much, as we drift
downstream, kids dispatched, canoes well-packed
and provisioned, some agitation, eddies say, our lives
like the rivers, the Madawaska, the French,
the surface placid, untroubled, happy couples all
on a trip, some currents underneath, of course,
watch out, tugging us one way and the other,
just look at that cliff, will you, the granite face of it,
the birches, pines, shit, our bright vessel banged up
against the rock you never saw, dimwit, our lives
like the Coulonge, the Noire, twisting, swerving,
doubling back from dead ends, you always do this,
turning a corner to narrow and explode, always,
asshole, through this churning bottleneck of rocks,
all our needs and secrets spilling forth, for Christ's sake,
in the rapids, and the wreck, the wreck of our lives.

Skating with Jane
(On Grenadier Pond)

Skates and toddlers piled in
with hockey stick,
we galumph sled down slope
to see how thick
the ice is, take a step
and test our weight.
Our boys can hardly walk,
let alone skate,
but the pond is a dare
we can't resist,
an equation we'll prove
only like this:
black, hard, smooth as mica.
You lace up fast
and race off to carve scratch
after white scratch
in this high-gloss tabletop.
I undo boots,
buckle up kiddie skates,
rearrange toques,
mitts, try to warm with words
their frozen hands,
then send them out onto
the bright expanse
we've got all to ourselves—
this adventure
that stretches clear to Queen,
touched here and there
with wisps and drifts of snow
the wind pushes

against their cheeks, across
the lake's dark surface,
the whole Breughelesque scene—
which you skate back
towards me on... And then—
then there's a crack
like a rifle going off,
an almighty PING
—sound of sheet metal
caught in the wind—
that ricochets around,
reverberates
over the lake and hums
beneath our blades.
You stopped; they tottered on.
I can't forget
your eyes exploding wide,
sure this was it,
the ice that held, that held,
the smile that spread—
no, broke across your face:
Holy shit, you said. Holy shit.

Herons on Ice

Having had their summer, swum, fished, plunged
in their chosen waters, these old birds
have awoken to find the world changed,
their prime stretch of pond frozen. And it hurts,

how it hurts these debonair gents
as they gamely pretend to get with the times,
to accept the ice, like old colonial lieutenants
returned to cold, foreign homes,

to hard, unyielding soil. One botches a landing,
wings akimbo in feathery consternation,
then slips off to repair her damaged standing.
Another, less given to self-laceration,

a wizened old cad adjusting his cravat,
ventures forth to assay the dance floor, a snappy new tune,
still sporting, years after the fact,
the regimental colours that made the ladies swoon.

Uncreaking his joints to an unfamiliar rhythm,
each tentative step's a stiff skid and jerk,
a disaster averted. Now only grief and ruin
can come of the ways that once charmed the world.

White Pine

1

You were young once, it's true, in some dark fin-de-siècle,
down a Gothic cul-de-sac, where coal-begrimed gargoyles
like malevolent uncles watched over you, and your bones
drew nourishment, drew calcium from the dirty loam,
the milk-white fibres growing strong, growing tall.
A strapping young sapling you were once, it's true.
But were you you? Or just another plank… straight and white?

2

Hard sometimes to believe we're all unique—
take a peak out the airplane porthole
at all those trees multiplying like stubble
across the earth's rugged face… Take another peak,
and take the snowflake: they now claim
each one, begotten in those Rubensesque
clouds of roly-poly white flesh,
comes out exactly the same,
perfect little crystals that tumble
into a world that buffets and breaks them
and their dreams, time and time again,
till they, like us, crash to earth,
each, a true, twisted original.

3

No wonder, once the slaughter in the trenches
knocked them for a loop, no wonder those city boys
headed north in their English suits to find
the skeletons they knew they hid inside,
to paint the truths they pined for, these figures
they saw limp from the woods, walking wounded,
outcasts, deserters, scarecrows, shellshocked vets
returning to take up positions,
imploring the heavens with upthrown arms,
defying the elements in a desperate stand
on a windswept point. But the further north they went,
canvas canoes packed with canvas and oils
they lugged from lake to lake, the more the shapes
they painted became the emblems, not of a time,
but of the place they invented:
revenant, shaman, wound, wilderness, pine.

4 *(from the Spanish)*

What moves me to love you, my lord,
is not the heaven you've promised;
nor is it the hell the church preaches
that moves me to follow you, your teaching.
You move me; the very sight of you
nailed to the cross and jeered at moves me;
it moves me to see the gashes in your sides,
to see you scorned, to see you die.
Most of all it's your love that moves me;
if there were no heaven, I would still adore you;
no hell, I would still be frightened of you.
Nothing you can do or give will change this:
even if I didn't wish for what I wish,
I'd love you the same as I do now, or more.

5

Out of such crooked timber, what straight thing
was ever made? The great white pines are gone
from the Saguenay, the Coulonge, the Dumoine;
you find them only at the fringes
in ones and twos, in out-of-the-way places,
retired to lick their wounds, to cultivate
their quirks: five needles like fingers,
a trunk with bark flaking off and gum
suppurating from each gash; the grain
swirling like sinews tensed round each knot,
each knot a branch stopped, lopped off,
each branch an arm, a tortured wish
to grasp a swift creature in flight,
some sweet morsel of passing life.

Stop. Start Again.

On the last day of the year, in the last year
of the century I was born in,
I went into the woods with my brothers.
It was cold, there was a wind,
and we skied hard to warm ourselves
and harder still as we raced, testing each other
the way we did when we were boys.
We skied through cedars and pines, up slopes
and down, one overtaking the others,
breezing past on the downhill, or poling
one's weight up, and bushwhacking around.
Then in a stand of hardwoods, we stopped
and stood, still as those trees, and caught our breath
as the last evening of the year arrived.
We stopped and stood and filled our lungs
and watched our breath drift
and with it, the words we spoke
that snowy evening, silver-white puffs of vapour
vanishing among the birches and maples,
the cloudy snow, the snow-laden sky.
All we could hear was the wind in the treetops,
sighing for one last leaf to rustle,
and silence, as though everything had frozen
and the woods, like an orchestra, had stopped.
And in that stillness a tree,
like a door easing open, creaked:
it was a trunk about to disclose its booty,
to unburden itself of heirlooms, and arthritis,
of hand-me-down recriminations and failures,
it was an old woman bemoaning the ache in her legs,
how she'd stood in line all these years for nothing,

a soldier recounting the long way he'd come
the wars he'd fought, and this, his only reward.
It was a story about to begin, new or old,
to turn into words in the silent woods.
And I thought, no, don't start, please don't.
We stood, the creaking stopped,
and then we started off again,
our skis imprinting their lines
in the uncomplaining snow, lines
that would be there, or gone, in the morning.

Different Pears

Midwinter: wondering what to serve
for dessert, I run my hand over a pear
at a stand in Kensington Market.
You've gone shopping for jeans, the one pair
you own too baggy. If the world was flat,
it would be easy to put on a map
but it curves, curves just the way
this turnip-hard Bosc does in my grip.
I look for Bartletts. They're stretch, says the girl,
Try a size smaller. You take one more pair
behind the curtain. How can we show
all sides of the globe on a flat surface?
These are Packhams from Argentina,
ample-bottomed, water-logged
and overripe. You're taking a while in there.
At the edges, a map always distorts,
stretching a little land over a lot
of surface. Here are the Bartletts.
You pull the waist tight and emerge.
The most precise projections cleave
the globe into two hemispheres
that curve down the page, like the hips
you spin before the mirror:
South Africa, South America. Let me feel:
these Anjou are just right. I'll take them.

Party Season
(25 Lines for December)

Tinsel-string, styro-snow—
up go the ornaments
along the downtown streets;
up yours, growls the panhandler
in Santa hat who's failed
to cadge his season's treats

from these slick tarts and spivs
spilling homeward after
another office drink.
It's grey, low-pressure weather:
the sky like a screen glows
momentarily blank

before new merchandise
moves in to deck the aisles
and dazzle us with pixels.
Your calendar fills up
and your head, you lament,
with a thud like wet cement.

Nature abhors a vacuum—
mulled wine, beer, eggnog, rum…
You don't know what you want.
When the first flakes finally come,
they'll be like spores of aspirin
spun, dissolving in a glass

of water: Joy at last.

End of Winter
(Whitehorse)

Late April: you can keep your porky gophers
popping up to check how long their shadows is—
Here, we got the real thing: snow from October
to May, weeks of minus fifty, or worse,
mornings you dive for the light switch first thing,
as life shrinks like a tunnel you can't see
the end of. Till you do. And it's spring:
Hans has the sled-dogs chained up by the creek,
and, as we dig ourselves out, you hear, no surprise,
that a flurry of googly-eyed couples
has gone splitsville… Those poor, pasty-faced guys
trying to get lucky just when the latest crop
of extreme-sports dudes blows into town,
bronzed, buff and gunning for serious fun.

Markham Street

Undo me, you asked, your back turned to me,
the clasp at the nape of your neck
a trick padlock to test intrepid fingers,
the dress all prelude and the party we'd been to
that night on Markham Street
still fizzing in our heads. It was fall,
the asphalt strewn with leaves we raced our bikes through,
escaping. The party went on, the leaves flew,
we laughed and didn't know what we'd do,
riding home, you to me, I to you,
in the years to come, all the places we'd make home
—this house now off Markham Street—
then turn around, my love, and leave—*click*—
the door open, the dress falling... Undo me. I did.

The Inbox

1

Dawn with a beep-beep you extinguish arrives
and this clunk-clunk-clunking you can't
of the Dundas streetcars as they shunt
their loads of worker bees to downtown hives,
smartphones humming, chirping shrill homilies
that worm into your ear: rise and shine,
the early bird gets the worm, time to grind
the coffee, to bathe and beauty your body,
to swathe yourself in officewear and face the music—
Oh there are emails in your inbox piling up,
underlings to dispatch, switches to flick,
whole factories waiting for your go-ahead
and frilly ribbons for you in your finery to snip...
Yes, and this paw on your vacillating hip.

2

Grow up, get real and be responsible—
your hip, my paw, your words.
Your hip under my paw—undermine.
I swear to tell the truth, the whole truth,
and nothing but, I say, hand palpitating
on the good book of your gracious thigh.
Of course, the joint chiefs will trumpet
the party line, spout the standard inanities
—grow up, get real, be responsible—
but the masses are already warming
to my gospel of peace and love triumphant,
down the flanks and in their hearts they know
there's no sense fighting these insurgents,
the tide has turned and so, my love, have you.

3

Face to face, the truth, and nothing but—
all those emails in your inbox piling up,
let them keep proclaiming, or not;
my gospel of peace and love I will preach
till the air turns blue, and all the schoolgirls
stream from their lunchrooms and boutiques
to join the movement, but the truth is,
as I scan your face and see through the years
I've known you, as I sink into your eyes
and see our shimmering limbs, and breathe,
and run my hands down your mottled back
and round your behind, your nothing but,
round and round the nub of it, the truth is
you raise a finger to my lips: *Ssshhh!*

4

Ssshhh! You implore your rowdy grade six boys
who titter at the run in your tights;
the girls, though, hear a crack in your voice
as you read—*Ssshhh!* I thought I heard the door,
the floorboards creak, you say, and freeze
in the middle of the bed—*Ssshhh!* We fly
across the thick, the thin black ice of the lake,
swooping, carousing, whooping till—*Ssshhh!*
the crack resounds, quavers beneath our skates
to die in your throat—*Ssshhh!* We sink, pale limbs
swallowed by the lake, we swish and flail
and disturb the starry surface, on which
you thought you felt a dark bird swim past
and heard—*ssshhh!*—a wet birth or death warble—*Ssshhh!*

5

Let us sleep and wake again, somewhere else—
let us be just flesh, pink-brown haunches
surfacing in the Georgian Bay's expanse
like spare parts from an orgy, smooth granite,
garnet-freckled, lichen-blemished, lolling
in the warm sun letting the water soothe
and lap each limb, torso, each curve, we could just
do what's natural, and nothing but,
loving only what looks and feels good,
nerves tingling, all flesh, pleasure accruing... We could—
if it weren't for these cracks in the rock
in which matter collects like doubts, like debts,
and these thoughts take root, striving upwards,
righteous little seedlings, spoiling our fun.

6

What'll we do when we're old, where'll we live,
what'll we eat? Cat food, dog food, under a bridge,
in a cardboard shack on a subway grate.
Eight a.m. The early-to-work office drones
have already dispatched their first salvo
of pension-plan updates to scare
the living daylights out of us poor saps,
and now kick back in their swivel chairs
to reap the benefits, spinning twizzle-sticks
round their lattes in ever-widening gyres.
And how your inbox groans with the weight
of things there are to worry over, the rates
you're forgoing, the interest you compound—
all that you're getting out of what I put in.

7

Let me reiterate. Bed is bad.
Work is where we need to go. Oh, oh, oh—
to work, my little fingers, to work.
Think, all those emails in your inbox piling up
one atop the other, to acquaint you
with our lowest rates, regale you
with little Johnny's latest grimace,
update you on the lamentable state
of this or that mistake, and so reinstate
if not berate, upgrade you
to our toughest anti-virus yet which will stop
all those emails slipping through your filter slots
as you lie in bed—let me reiterate—
blissfully receptive and unprotected.

8

Tap tap tap. Reiter—iterate away.
The woodpecker outside our window
sinks his beak into a leafless tree.
He's your kind of go-to guy, banging home
his point as he tries to digitize
the nuggets he's picked up: Rise and shine, early bird.
Go get that worm before he turns. Too late.
The good book of your gracious hips, that volume
with its warm mass colliding in the bed,
has loosed the word and turned the worm, turned you—
let the streetcars go on shunting their loads
to the city's heart, let the workers disperse
to their cubicles and monitors,
let the emails in your inbox overflow.

In Tadoussac
(for Briony Glassco)

1

You scan the steel-blue surface for a hint, a disturbance,
that might take the shape you want. Waves heave and jos-
tle and keep coming, so many you can hardly keep track,
throwing up whitecaps that resolve into suds and sea wash,
not the slick black solid mass you want, fin or flank. And
the more intently you look, the more time you invest, the
more certain you grow you'll see one. Oh, they're out there
for sure, the old salt insists. Plenty of them in the sea.
What was that? A log? Some debris? Just a rogue wave the
sea has swallowed. You keep looking, keep staring. There!
There! There! They come so fast you don't know what you're
seeing. Until finally you decide there's nothing—they're all
just waves and they're laughing at you.

2

No. You saw something—what? You started with an idea
of what you would see, some fabulous beast, and you're
waiting till it appears. Was that it? Just a glimpse. You'll
have to wait some more, and the more you wait, suspended
as the boat rocks, in the lull before the next sighting, the
more fabulous the creature grows. Was it hair you saw? Or
a hip? You're like a new lover: unsure in the extreme, ner-
vous system tingling, ready to imagine anything.

3

You saw nothing, and now it's night, you go to bed and close your eyes. Slipping beneath the surface, you sense dark masses displacing themselves. A warm flank. A hump slowly breaching. Was that a tail raised, the mist from a sudden spout lingering? In the morning, the sheets ripple and seal the evidence.

Not Unmarried

Not unmarried, no, just a little dis—
you smile—connected. Oh? Your eyes meet hers,
dip, then slip away, down cheek and blouse, scared
to see what they might say. How to explain this?
Last night the sheets like a glacier lay
between me and the one who shares my bed.
Her eyes have fixed on you, you feel the glare
and daren't look back. Not yet. It was too late
to set out, to risk another rebuff.
The sun's last rays still reached—what can she think?—
the high, forbidding peaks and in the folds below
the night turned blue. Should you raise your eyes up?
You do. She laughs. She hasn't heard a thing.
She toys with her wine, and then toys with you.

Not Drunk

–I wouldn't say he was… –Him? Never.
–But he'd had a few. –One or two.
–He was in a good mood. And hearty too.
–Hail fellow well met? –It was a good day.
–And he was ready for it. – Lubricated?
–Well-oiled and well-fuelled.
–His tank was full. So were his sails.
Jib, mainsail, spinnaker billowing
five sheets to the wind
and what a head of steam he had.
–Unstoppable. –Unquenchable.
–So he'd got his sea-legs back?
–Back so fast he'd lost them again
just the way he had his land-legs.
–Couldn't walk? –He's very good on all fours.
–Could he talk? –Not the way we do right now
with words and language and such,
but he could make himself understood.
–I see. –He was at one with the world.
–Do you mean he was over the limit,
out cold and incapacitated?
–I can think of better ways to put it.

Adulterous Mannequins

Having discovered they're—guess what?—in love,
they find hotels to pass the night, business trips,
broken-down vehicles, the usual pretexts,
and, in a strip-mall's dim café, breakfast
on mangos and kiwis. Indulge them, please.
They've discovered something new, unheard of,
a continent, or star no one else has glimpsed.
Feelings, of course, will need to be expressed
and words, poor words, won't do them justice.
Let them stride out on the boulevard
and catch fresh incarnations of themselves
in the plate-glass windows, as they trace
the flutterings of their souls, each whim and shift,
with these long looks and angles of the wrist.

Cracks in the Granite

1: Schamhaar

We could be just flesh and reckless pleasure,
lolling like these reefs we lie and dry on,
if it weren't for the cracks in the granite,
little worry-lines, wrinkles, troughs that mar
the perfectly tanned surface and show the age
of this ancient rock. Look how the shadows
and moisture collect there, how the moss
caulks those seams with green velvet and swells,
and now how these bushes take root and sprout,
tender shoots of juniper and blueberry,
crouching at first to avoid detection
as they advance, conquering new territory,
a growth, a scourge, this prickly underbrush
rising from the depths to resist my touch.

2: Bush Talk

A crack, a crevice that to escape the touch
of your fingers, your tongue, plunges straight down
through the bedrock, piercing granite to tap
and release what's deep inside, to let
the soft jelly of the self exhale its fumes
and vapours, its inchoate aspirations—
If only we could say what we want!
And in delineating our desires,
make them come true, our words becoming fact,
tangible matter, the way this little bush
emerges from the rock, a wisp of utterance
hardening into roots and stalk, sentences
stretching into branches, each teeny leaf
a tongue to name some flesh, some new pleasure.

3: Giving Up the Ghost

Or think of those early Christian paintings,
so crude and endearing, some battlefield
or plague-ridden city, the priest and family
attending the recumbent lord or knight,
administering last rites, or washing feet,
or mopping brow, as he quite literally
gives up the ghost—which is to say, his soul,
depicted here as mere breath, a speech bubble
exiting the mouth and rising buoyantly
to the heavens. Now look at the hole
it came out of. Does it wince? Does it smile
as it releases this last puff of hope?
Poor forsaken mouth, open gash, slit, crack,
only now—slack, mute, unfed—can you heal.

Long Time No See
(in memory of Carmen Campos)

As if zipping out of some early Italian film
and into this sun-ravaged seaside town,
as if on a Vespa, you arrive
and dismount, nifty, radiant, *desenvuelta*,
flashing a grin—it's been some vacation—
your voice all mockery and surprise:

                                        Twenty years!
Tell me everything, I want to ask—the full account—
as you shed your sunglasses, the truths you've gleaned,
the places, the joys you've discovered... No, don't—
Let me look in your eyes and see what you've seen.

Little Louis and the Big Sea

Wait for me, he cries,
as the big kids, the swimmers,
charge off to toss themselves in the surf,
to vanish and, like dolphins, re-emerge.

Wait for me, he howls,
louder and more desperate now,
and only the sea listens,
waits like a cat to be stroked or to pounce;

each purr a new wave that appears,
each wave a paw stretching
further up the sand, baring its white claws,
and swiftly pulling back.

Last week a German girl was drowned
and down the beach an Arab prince
constructs watchtowers and mosques,
whole Alhambras of sand

this sea will rip apart. A ring round his middle,
Louis tries the water, and retreats
to puzzle, silent, over
the catastrophe howling at his feet.

The Family Car

"Ah, no, the years, oh!"
                    —Thomas Hardy

The four of us in the family car again,
each taking his place
and she, hers at the steering wheel:
behind her, one boy reads,
the other eyes the scenery, or sleeps.
In front, I tweak the radio,
check the map, navigate and so,
as usual, each in his spot,
and she in hers,
on our weekly rounds, we go:
to soccer, to hockey,
to someone's for dinner,
to all the things that fill our evenings
and our lives:
to find snow at Christmas
or start the summer,
trunk and plans packed to overflow,
the highway unzipping ahead,
as the years go by—ah, no, the years, oh!

And now we drive home in the car again,
each back in his place,
and she, in hers (she sighs).
The boy behind her grows,
just grows, like a weed,
knees jabbing the small of her back,
as he devours his read;

the other talks of things he's seen or heard
and some that trouble him
—Where will this animal or man
sleep tonight, and what eat?—
and home we putter,
from soccer and supper, Christmas and summer,
till the car and we grow old,
till we cough and sputter,
joints ache and creak, brakes squeak,
till our bodies give out, and we up and go,
as the junkyard calls: ah, no, the years, oh!

Tamarack
(for Ricardo Sternberg)

We've come too late: the oak and maple leaves,
thick underfoot, like the hoofprints
of some wild herd that stomped and partied all night,
then vanished to leave a few bright leaflets
littered on the trampled ground,
gaudy flyers advertising the bash we missed—

*

Their parents, though, have remained behind
to supervise: a stand of stalwart hardwoods,
sober-suited as bankers in their grey bark,
pillars of the community, responsible, upright
as a barcode we scan—

*

                              And through them catch
the hardy unrepentant green
of hemlock, fir, cedar, spruce and pine,
huddled in bands like true believers,
holding on to their principles and needles,
ready to tough it out all winter—

*

And in among them one artful infiltrator
with the truest name of all, straight As,
—either pure Scots, Ojibway or both—
this fellow traveller that plays along,
green when it's cool to be green
but when it gets cold, like it did last week,
all his needles turn mango-yellow,
turn gold, and tumble to the ground
just as he hightails it out of town. Tamarack.

Camping

The excitement! A swathe of soft coppery cedar
and pine needles between two trees and the canoe
we've pulled up, one boy testing for rocks
and protruding roots, first on hands and knees,
then flat on his back, miming sleep,
announces, delighted, he's found the spot.
His brother, older, now unrolls the tent,
stretching out the corners and, serious
as the doctor who gave him his shots,
inserts the pegs. Later, as the last wisps rise
from the firepit, we'll sink into sleeping bags,
ears pricked for each twig that snaps, the shadows
climbing up the walls of our nylon cave,
the Great Bear beyond arranging our fate.

Driving West

Though it's half-empty, this bus barrelling west,
ploughing, skipping through towns, gearing up, down,
can't outrace the dark. Across the aisle,
a young mother wrestles with her restless child
who wants to know why this, why that;
behind a grim old couple sit, resigned
to saying not a word
lest they give the wrong impression.
You and the usual riff-raff
scatter yourselves and possessions
over aisle and window seats. Ahead
the sun sets, its slow explosion spread
across the driver's dark glasses—
you'll face the end at this angle,
oblique, diagonal,
putting your book aside to look
out the window, to let the landscape
come at you: lakes, hardwood stands,
cedar swamps, beaver dams,
pasture cleared and marked with split-rail fences,
marred by rocky outcrops,
motels abandoned, fruit stands shuttered for the night,
a Baptist church, a zinc-steepled Catholic one,
and houses, yes, houses: the old clapboard kind
with paint flaking off the weathered planks,
a rusty red swing set outside,
the new brick or vinyl-sided bungalows
each on its patch of precious lawn,
a shiny pickup parked in the drive.
People, it seems, work and retire here, carving lives
out of the woods behind their lot,

stringing hobbies and possessions
along the road for all to see.
You keep peering out as if waiting,
searching for a character, just one inhabitant,
to reappear in your book, to show up,
own up to this world. No such luck.
Did the last bus through spirit everyone away?
It's the magic hour: the light
seems to come not from the sky
but out of objects themselves—
the outer leaves of a maple glow
as though it were one huge lightbulb. You stare
and now the next tree starts to darken from the core,
night spreading from the trunk
out along the branches and twigs
to the leaves... You stare: it's dark
except for the oily blue sky
in this forsaken, irradiated land
where the horizon glows and everyone has gone...
Are you in the bus the last ones left?
Someone mumbles urgently down their phone,
then, across the aisle, there's a bustle and click
as the boy flicks on an overhead light:
the dark you've been staring into
has suddenly become a face:
grizzled cheeks, dishevelled hair, shifty eyes
you apprehend, and can't escape... It's you, it's me,
caught off-guard—*nur ein trüber Gast*—
seeker, pale ghost—*auf der dunklen Erde*—
shimmering a moment on the darkened earth.

Funeral Home

Across the street from the hospital,
so obvious and faux-respectable
we paddle right by it, like a frog
on a lily pad, biding its time
waiting for flies, for us, the funeral home.
That's right, just across from the hospital,
the paramedics and the hardcore cases
dragging their drip-trolleys out
to sneak a sad, defiant puff.
Just going in for a spell, we thought,
a night or two to get our counts back up
before winter, and our energy,
but some of us, well, never step back
through those revolving doors.
We end up down a different corridor
dealing with another order of business:
Imagine the owner going in to discuss
his start-up loan, the site picked,
glossy business plan in a binder,
the phrases he chose to pitch it
—*steady earner, constant influx*—
and the bank manager, nodding, nodding,
lunch coming up, some old friend
who's been sick, say, she stands,
ignoring the fat package, all the work
this guy did, surplus apostrophes buzzing
around his laborious words,
ushering him out, yes, already decided, yes,
with a hand that might be shooing a fly.
Then, months later, it's summer,
a cruel twist, sudden choices
to be made, and here she is, a new customer.

Deft Twist

The way you left—abrupt,
smart, like the salute
the soldiers of your childhood gave
or the stop a skater might execute
to spray us with ice—except
you were stopping and skating away,
leaving, so it was just that deft
little twist you gave your wrist
to keep the canoe you soloed off
on course, the paddle-blade
turned keel a second or two,
sinking in to steer you straight
—you who always knew the way—
then slipping silently out
of the water as you pull it back,
hardly a ripple or scratch
on the surface, only these drops
running down the blade
and tumbling from the tip,
one after another, not blood,
not ink, no, just peas in a pod,
four boys between gunwales,
heading off on another trip,
except you're alone now,
and these drops are just drops that drip
from your still paddle. They don't stop.

Cornstalks

Poking through the snow
of late March, through the crust
of ice the bright sun melts
and glances off, the cornstalks

ploughed under last fall
rise like broken bones—
rows and rows of them, bleached
and hollow, like limbs thrown

up in horror and promptly
sundered, with here and there
a husk the wind tugs at,
a telltale wisp of lemony-white hair.

Tall poppies cut down to size,
a platoon of ragtag
soldiers struggling through the mud
to plant a tattered flag

on fields far from this one,
how easy it is to make them,
brittle and fallen as they are,
speak of pain and devastation.

But come night when the moon bathes
in an otherworldly glow
this field, let them release
from each dark hollow

the dreams they harbour—
let them be the bent elbows
and outstretched arms of swimmers
parting far oceans,

lines and lines of runic script
celebrating the genealogies
and gory deeds of mythic beasts,
the stick figures of refugees

who, arriving at passport control,
unload as fast as
they can their jokes and puns,
and fall about themselves laughing,

before marching,
as they must at dawn,
into a new realm,
single-minded and solemn.

Joni and the Job Done

He's been tree-planting up north for two months
and is back with a new swagger
about his shoulders and red beard, all toughened up
at having taken the measure of himself
and the country, hauled his young body out of
sleeping bags and tents, through railway towns,
trucker stops, bars, innumerable clearcuts,
carousing with his crew, these rowdy girls and boys
he hugs goodbye at the roadside with those arms
that have embraced it all—the bugs, the bags—
and hoist his pack once more. Now he gets in the car.
There's an old Joni Mitchell CD out
and, to my surprise, this boy
who's always mocked the music I play says,
play that song. I like it. And as I play it,
the song I used to listen to at his age,
for him now, I imagine how he first heard it
and came to like it, some cold night in camp,
in someone's tent, perhaps, and the whole next day
humming it as he stomps through the clear-cut,
sinks his shovel, twists the handle, plops a seedling in,
tamps down the soil with his toe, takes two steps
and does it all again, the same five actions
he'll repeat two or three thousand times a day,
ten cents a tree, in his steel-toed boots,
Muskol and sunscreen mixing with sweat
at his hairline to form a residue
that will stay with him all summer, like this song
he hums about needing to leave someone you like,
and the clean white linen he misses because Joni does,
or did, and makes us feel that we do too. Poor Joni,

who's rich now, but can't walk, can't talk, it seems;
Joni who got pregnant at twenty and came east,
where no one knew her, to have her baby
one winter in a Yorkville rooming house,
working at Eaton's to pay the rent,
to be a singer, to sing so that Malcolm,
who's also twenty, can stomp through the clearcut,
shovel-twist-tree-tamp-tromp, humming her tune,
thinking maybe he, too, will be rich soon
after all the trees he's planted this summer,
and there are so many things he can do,
so many places he can go, maybe
he'll go to Amsterdam, maybe Rome,
maybe he'll buy a fancy bike and ride
round Europe, see the canals, the Colosseum,
or go to Greece, sleep on the beach, he thinks
as he comes up a crest and a deer, startled,
veers off, tail bobbing, into the trees.
And as we drive off, I imagine Joni
that winter in Toronto, alone, decided,
smiling, amid tears and blood, at the baby
she's about to give up and thinking perhaps
the same thing I do with this young man beside me
who's all grown up and hums her song,
who'll need to leave soon: "There, that job's done."

Last Paddle

Supper done and the August sun
about to go, the two of you
subtract yourselves from kitchen,
from dishes and grandchildren,
to take the blue canoe
out for one last paddle
round our summer sites,
these swimming rocks and heron swamps
north of Pointe-au-Baril.
There's a lurch and a curse
as you embark, old antagonists
always ready to go
another round, to skirmish
as the canoe wobbles,
to spar over ancient foibles
or a loon that's just popped up,
then laugh it off like drops
off a duck's back, splish-splash,
resuming your old truce
with gentle, rhythmic strokes
and the laughter I hear echo
over the glowing water
as I stand and watch you go—
the two of you in silhouette
in the blue canoe, now black,
just an outline that merges into
the dark islands, their ragged skyline
of wind-tormented pines,
and re-emerges, as the sun
consumes itself behind,
yellow and orange and blazing red,

and the two of you paddle on,
paddle out towards the open,
the great big Georgian Bay—there,
there's no troublesome strip
of earth to get in the way,
no horizon left to hold you back,
no more pain, or sorrow,
no ego, it's all washed away
in mist, in this grey-white glow
the lake climbs right into the sky,
as I stand and watch you go,
your canoe just a speck
in the silver distance,
the whirls from your paddles
undoing, unspooling like thoughts,
or sentences trailing off
on the lake's metallic surface,
little galaxies that spin
and expend themselves
and vanish into the dark,
in which, having stood and watched
you subtract yourselves from us,
I see nothing but you gone—
you are the darkness you've left
and the evening's first faint star.

Don't Ask

And when, my fellow ephemeral blip,
not just you but the whole leaking ship,
the show we thought would run and run,
spins, like a top, to its end, like a stone
through the stony-faced planets drops,
what, oh, what then? Think of the man-hours you've spent
at your post, plugging away pen in hand
while the world plunged. Think of the cathedrals
those craftsmen took centuries to build,
the glorious vaults they'd start and never live
to see completed, the roofs now dispersing slate by slate,
falling to pieces, tumbling through the ether,
piano keys, blank pages, scraps of notepaper,
all like snowflakes into black water... And your words,
when it goes, when it all goes,
and you've long since taken your leave,
little believer, will they really pitter-patter
across the eardrums of an expiring soldier,
fizzle on the screen of some faraway monitor?

Acknowledgements

The Antigonish Review: "Markham Street," "The Inbox 1-5"
Contemporary Verse 2: "Herons on Ice," "Skating with Jane"
Fiddlehead: "Dark Woods"
Global Poetry Anthology 2015 (Montreal International
    Poetry Prize): "Funeral Home"
Literary Review of Canada: "Not Unmarried"
The Walrus: "Artichoke"
Vallum: "Don't Ask"

For their help and patience with these poems, I am grateful
to Deborah Lambie, Ricardo Sternberg, Carmine Starnino,
Nyla Matuk, Christopher Clark, Mark Migotti, Don Coles,
Carolyn Smart, Richard Murphy, and Clyde Sanger.

My editor Zach Wells was extraordinarily committed and
uncompromising—hands-on and hard-ass—and I am
very grateful to him.

About the Author

PHOTO: RITA LEISTNER

Richard Sanger has published two previous collections of poetry, *Shadow Cabinet* and *Calling Home*, both with Signal Editions. His poems have appeared in many publications in Canada, Britain, and the United States, including *London Review of Books* and *Poetry Review*. His plays include *Not Spain*, *Two Words for Snow*, *Hannah's Turn*, and *Dive* as well as translations of Calderon, Lorca, and Lope de Vega. He has also published essays, reviews, and poetry translations. He lives in Toronto.